Yellow Umbrella Books are published by Capstone Press
151 Good Counsel Drive, P.O. Box 669, Mankato, Minnesota 56002
http://www.capstone-press.com

Library of Congress Cataloging-in-Publication Data
Trumbauer, Lisa, 1963–
      Families/by Lisa Trumbauer.
      p. cm.
      Includes index.
      ISBN 0-7368-0734-9
      1. Family. [1. Family.] I. Title.
HQ744.T69   2001
306.85—dc21   00-036672

      Summary: Describes different types of families, what family members do together, and
      where families live.

Editorial Credits:
Susan Evento, Managing Editor/Product Development; Elizabeth Jaffe, Senior Editor;
      Jessica Maldonado, Designer; Kimberly Danger and Heidi Schoof, Photo Researchers

Photo Credits:
Cover: Photo Network/Bachmann; Title Page: Photo Network/Tom McCarthy Photos; Page 2:
Photo Network/Myrleen Ferguson Cate, Photo Network/Michael Philip Manheim (inset);
Page 3: Photri-Microstock (top), Pictor (bottom); Page 4/5: Photri-Microstock (spread); Page 4:
Photo Network/Bachmann (inset); Page 5: Pictor (inset); Page 6: Unicorn Stock Photos/Tom
McCarthy (top), Photo Network/Bachmann (bottom); Page 7: Photo Network /Bill Lai (top),
Pictor (bottom); Page 8: Thomas Kitchin/TOM STACK & ASSOCIATES (left), Visuals
Unlimited/Mark E. Gibson (right); Page 9: Visuals Unlimited/Mark E. Gibson (left), Photo
Network/Robert Ginn (right); Page 10: Unicorn Stock Photos/Tom McCarthy (left),
International Stock/Dick Dickinson (right); Page 11: Shaffer Photography/James L. Shaffer
(left), Bob Daemmrich/Pictor (right); Page 12: Pictor; Page 13: Shaffer Photography/James L.
Shaffer (top right), Photri-Microstock (bottom left); Page 14: Pictor (top left), Photo
Network/Bachmann (bottom right); Page 15: Shaffer Photography/James L. Shaffer; Page 16:
Unicorn Stock Photos/Tom McCarthy

1 2 3 4 5 6 06 05 04 03 02 01

Families

by Lisa Trumbauer

Consulting Editor: Gail Saunders-Smith, Ph.D.
Consultants: Claudine Jellison and
Patricia Williams, Reading Recovery Teachers
Content Consultant: Andrew Gyory, Ph.D., American History

Yellow Umbrella Books

an imprint of Capstone Press
Mankato, Minnesota

All families are made up of people.

Some families are big.
Some families are small.

Some families are made up
of mothers, fathers, brothers,
sisters, grandparents, aunts,
uncles, cousins, and pets!

Families also can be made up of special friends.

Who is in your family?

Families look different.

What does your family look like?

Families need a place to live.
Some families live in
apartments. Other families
live in houses.

In what other places can families live?

People in families work.
Some people build houses.
Some people work in offices.

Families work together
to take care of one another.
Families also work together
to take care of their homes.

Families have fun together!
Some families like to hike.

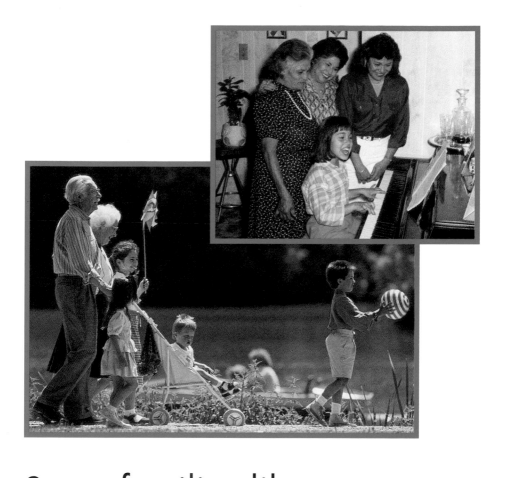

Some families like
to sing together.
Some families like
to go to the park together.

Some families like
to play games together.

Some families like
to read together.
How does your family
have fun together?

What is your family like?

Words to Know/Index

apartment—a group of rooms in which people live; apartments are usually part of a larger building; page 8

aunt—a sister of someone's mother or father; page 4

cousin—a daughter or son of someone's aunt or uncle; page 4

friend—a person whom someone knows well and enjoys being with; page 5

grandparent—a parent of someone's mother or father; page 4

hike—a long walk, especially in the country or in the forest; page 12

office—a room or building where people work; page 10

pet—a tame animal kept for company or pleasure; page 4

special—important and valuable; page 5

together—with one another; pages 11, 12, 13, 14, 15

uncle—a brother of someone's father or mother; page 4

Word Count: 158
Early-Intervention Levels: 9–12